To Our Readers:

INTRODUCING

OTABIND®

INTERNATIONAL

"The Book That Lies Flat"
— *User Friendly Binding* —

This title has been bound using state-of-the-art **OtaBind®** technology.

- The spine is 3-5 times stronger than conventional perfect binding
- The book lies open flat, regardless of the page being read
- The spine floats freely and remains crease-free even with repeated use

We are pleased to be able to bring this new technology to our customers.

Health Communications, Inc.

3201 S.W. 15th Street
Deerfield Beach, FL 33442-8190
(305) 360-0909

OTABIND®

INTERNATIONAL

The Netherlands

Praise for Tom Brady's
Sobriety Program

"I do not know of any work as adequate, as skilled, as lucid or as comprehensive as this one in guiding those who guide alcoholics toward sobriety, health and holiness."

M. Scott Peck, M.D., best-selling author of
A Road Less Traveled

". . . excellent material. Brady is quite specific and down-to-earth and I think that those who teach and follow his course will be able to get a good deal of value from his material."

Albert Ellis, Ph.D., Institute For
Rational-Emotive Therapy

THIRSTING FOR WHOLENESS
The Spiritual Journey Of
Addiction And Recovery

TOM BRADY, JR.

Health Communications, Inc.
Deerfield Beach, Florida

The Twelve Steps are reprinted with permission of Alcoholics Anonymous World Services, Inc. Permission to reprint and adapt the Twelve Steps does not mean that AA has reviewed or approved the contents of this publication nor that AA agrees with the views expressed herein. AA is a program of recovery from alcoholism — use of the Twelve Steps in connection with programs and activities which are patterned after AA, but which address other problems, does not imply otherwise.

Library of Congress Cataloging-in-Publication Data

Brady, Tom, Thirsting for wholeness: the spiritual journey of addiction and recovery / Tom Brady, Jr.
   p. cm.
   Includes bibliographical references.
   ISBN 1-55874-209-3
   1. 12-step programs — Religious aspects. 2. Spiritual formation. 3. Substance abuse — Religious aspects. 4. Compulsive behavior — Religious aspects. I. Title.
   BJ1596.B73 1992   91-40522
   248.8'6—dc20   CIP

©1992 Tom Brady, Jr.
ISBN 1-55874-209-3

Publisher: Health Communications, Inc.
             3201 S.W. 15th Street
             Deerfield Beach, Florida 33442-8190

Cover Design by Iris T. Slones

 # DEDICATION

To Harry, who lovingly and
unerringly guided me through the
initial stages of my journey
to recovery.

CONTENTS

INTRODUCTION

Addiction is a monumental problem in our society. Indeed, when we consider the ramifications of addiction, we might well conclude that it is our number-one health problem. Many thousands of people die from addiction each year, our prisons are overflowing with those convicted of drug-related crimes and hospital beds contain an alarming number of patients who are there because of alcohol, drug or other addictions. And that is not all. Many of those who are most harmed are family members — the husbands, wives, parents and children of those who are addicted. The families of addicts become as addicted to the addicts as the addicts are to their drug of choice. In response to their behavior, families adopt and live unhealthy, reactive lives and suffer horribly in the process. Friends, too, are caught up in the terrible cycle. As a matter of fact, anyone who cares about an addict in any way is vulnerable. Yet in spite of the enormity of the problem, there is apparently still little understanding of it.

Due mainly to misinformation or lack of knowledge, most addicts will continue to die of addiction, fill our prisons and take up an amazing number of hospital beds. Likewise, families and friends will continue to suffer. This realization is very sad, for this terrible process does not have to continue.

I know, beyond the shadow of any doubt, that addicts who come to discern the true nature of their illness can recover if they want to, provided they are given the proper guidance. The same is true for their families. All of them can experience happiness and have full, rich and meaningful lives. Many thousands of addicts and their families testify to these facts.

Perhaps addiction is not well understood because it is such a complex illness. Opinions about its nature vary widely, which further complicates the matter and adds to the confusion. Then, too, the different ideas about the disease lead to significantly different recommended modes of treatment and notions about recovery.

Through all this chaos, however, there shines a light of clarity. This light originated with some alcoholics who came to understand addiction in a simple way, discovered a mode of treatment that really worked and proceeded to recover from alcoholism. This light has since been passed on to millions of others, and it continues to shine as a beacon of hope, cutting through the chaotic darkness of complication and confusion.

This book is about addiction and recovery. It is about the search for God and others through addiction, and the finding of both through recovery. It represents my attempt to share some of the light that has been passed on to me. In it, I will emphasize the ideas of those who discovered the light, because I believe there is no substitute for personal experience in arriving at the truth. For instance, ophthalmologists may be able to tell you a great deal about blindness, but they cannot tell you what it is like to be blind. Only a blind person can tell you about this.

Those alcoholics who were enlightened eventually formed groups that had one purpose — recovery from alcoholism for themselves and for others. In time, these groups came to be called 12-Step groups since their program of recovery consisted of twelve steps. From the very beginning, these communities of recovering alcoholics stressed the primary importance of spirituality in both the illness of addiction and the recovery from it. In spite of this the fundamental role played by spirituality remains the least understood part. I am convinced that the very essence of addiction and recovery is spiritual. Because of this, throughout this book I will emphasize the role of spirituality.

This book is not another how-to manual, nor is it a scholarly work. And even though I use some of my personal experiences, it will not be the story of my recovery. It is simply my attempt to share with you, in a simple way, some reflections on the nature of addiction and recovery that I have found to be very useful.

If 12-Step groups have demonstrated anything, it is that there is incredible power in the sharing of personal experiences. Through such sharing, many who think they are different realize they are not, identify themselves as addicts, and join with sister and brother addicts on the road to health and wholeness.

To my alcoholic readers, let me say that my use of the words addict and addiction has a purpose. It enables me to address all addicts, their families, their friends and others regardless of what the addiction may be. Thus, it will enable me to reach more who have the illness, who are affected by it or who deal with it. I use these broad and convenient terms with reluctance for I am well aware that our society discounts the use of alcohol, which is its primary drug of choice, by paying maximum attention to other drugs. Only tobacco kills more people than alcohol but it, too, has been an historic favorite and has been, until recently, left alone to do its killing. Happily this is changing as people become more aware of the dangers involved in using tobacco.

To my female readers, I want to say that I know addiction is an equal opportunity illness that can destroy all its victims, female or male. Thus, be assured that my frequent use of the third-person masculine singular is purely for convenience.

Finally, this book is not the alpha and omega on the subject of addiction and recovery. I only know what I know, and that's all that I know, and I am aware that I have much more to learn. After all, learning is what life is about. However, I do believe that what I know is worth sharing with you, and this belief has been strengthened by many people who have urged me to write what I have said in various talks over the years.

It is my wish that this book will help broaden the knowledge of the illness of addiction for many, assist others in beginning the process of spiritual growth, give those already on the path some helpful insights and aid everyone who wants it in the adventure of becoming like a little child again.

Whatever your reaction might be, what I have written is my gift to you. I give it to you as it has been given to me since I began my own pilgrimage of recovery more than 26 years ago — with love. So, if you will, receive it in the spirit with which it is given.

Tom Brady, Jr.

PART ONE

The Journey

1

The Pathway Home

It has been said that life is a journey on which we may choose from many different paths. Some spiritual teachers have said that life is a circular pilgrimage because we all return to the precise point at which we started, no matter which path we take. For some, life seems to be only a matter of time and distance. Like Methuselah, they live and they die.

For others, however, life must be more than mere existence.

Something deep inside them cries out for more. These are the thirsty ones. The thirst that they feel is not physical, it is spiritual. It is an inner craving for the wholeness that comes through union with others and with God. Such thirst can be quenched only through the formation of loving relationships that produce the "at-one-ness" their spirits desire. If they find, choose and walk the path that satisfies their thirst, they will return to their point of origin also, but they will have their own rooms in the Father's house. They, like Enoch, will walk with God.

3

Among the thirsty ones, we find poets, musicians, artists, philosophers, writers, religious — and addicts. Yes, addicts. Although it may surprise some, my experience has clearly shown that addicts are among the most spiritually thirsty people in the world. As a matter of fact, the old name for alcoholism, dipsomania, means "crazy with thirst," and alcoholics satisfy their thirst with a substance that has been called "spirits." Ironic? Yes. Yet others have believed, and I agree, that all addictions have their beginnings in spiritual thirst.

Carl Jung, in a letter to Bill W., co-founder of Alcoholics Anonymous, wrote the following concerning an alcoholic he had treated:

> "His craving for alcohol was the equivalent, on a low level, of
> the spiritual thirst of our being for wholeness . . . union with
> God."[1]

The use of alcohol and drugs and some euphoria-producing behaviors is a pathway that millions of people mistakenly choose, thinking it will lead them to freedom and happiness. Then to their dismay, many of them realize that it has led them into the most desperate bondage, into the slavery of addiction.

The tragedy is that so many addicts die of addiction without ever finding real fulfillment. The good news is that more and more of them are discovering the highway to freedom, happiness and contentment. They are choosing and walking the path of recovery. And they are realizing that recovery is leading them to wholeness, quenching their thirst and fulfilling their deepest needs.

Recovery is a process that moves along a specific path. That path is spiritual growth. I am convinced that the only way to a happy, meaningful sobriety is through spiritual growth. Spiritual growth is essentially an inner journey that manifests itself in radical outer change. Some choose it eagerly and willingly. Others, including most addicts, choose it as a last resort, when there is no alternative.

However the choice is made, those who make it become the heroes of life. Guided by the principles that are basic to spiritual growth, they make the hero's journey, returning to their own innermost selves, to their rooms in the Father's house.

The Child Within

Spiritual growth is not understood by most people. Yet without being taught, little children seem to understand it and to know its basic principles. They are wise and eminently sensible. Perhaps it is because they are closer to the Source. Whatever the reason may be, little children automatically and naturally practice certain precepts in their daily lives.

For example, two of the fundamental principles of all spiritual paths are the recognition and acceptance of personal powerlessness and turning to a Higher Power for help. Children seem to embody these two principles. They intuitively know their limits, and any time they sense they are beyond those limits, they seek help from someone bigger than themselves. They don't have to think about it. Their reaction is automatic, instinctual.

Although we grow up, the child within us still knows its limits and exactly what to do when it is beyond them. This is why we find ourselves automatically turning to a Higher Power when we realize that a situation is beyond our control. I remember a dear friend of mine sharing an experience that illustrates this point well.

My friend was an atheist, or so he thought, yet he told me that when he was in a foxhole on a tiny Pacific island during World War II, and the bombs and shells began coming in, he discovered that he was praying, "Oh, God, please help me!" This he did in spite of the fact that he had never before prayed in his life! Something in him knew what to do, where to turn. So it is.

No matter how old we grow, there remains a child within us who has certain knowledge, and it is on this kind of knowledge that spiritual principles are based. This knowledge is not learned. It is intuitive. And in times of danger, it is remembered. It is an inner wisdom that ensures our survival and facilitates our growth.

Spiritual teachers have held that this kind of wisdom resides not in the head, but in the heart. Some people today equate the heart with the unconscious mind. Wherever it may be located, this deepest form of knowledge is natural and practical, is shared by all human beings and represents the rudiments of faith. Above all, it is what has always been known as "common sense."

Mystics

Little children are not alone in their intuitive grasp of spiritual principles. They are joined by another group, those who are called mystics. They, like children, seem to be closer to the Source. In spite of what some may think, most mystics are not far-out, wild-eyed misfits. On the contrary, most of them are among the sanest and wisest members of the human race. Mystics are usually very efficient, highly effective people, whose lives are filled with serenity, joy and service to others.

Jesus and the Buddha were mystics, and although they did not conform to the conventions of their time and were thus considered by some to be strange troublemakers, history has been mightily influenced by their teachings.

One modern mystic was Thomas Merton, whose books have inspired and enlightened many people. Whatever their differences, mystics are primarily concerned about relationships with other people, some Higher Power, the world of nature and the universe, and each of them has concentrated on gaining knowledge, not from the outer world, but from the innermost part of their being.

This innermost part has been called God within, the divine spark, the indwelling Christ, the child within and many other names. I call it the Knower. Regardless of what it is called, it seems to be a reservoir of spiritual wisdom that is in some way directly connected with God and made of the same stuff as God.

William James, the pragmatic philosopher/psychologist, called this innermost part of our being the "germinal higher part" of man that is intimately connected with "a MORE of the same quality, which is operative in the universe outside of him, and which he can keep in working touch with . . . ."[2]

One mystic, Meister Eckhart, wrote of this innermost part, "The seed of God is in us."[3] And a modern man has written: "I believe the inner child is a reservoir of strength, a repository of our best intuitions, and ultimate link to all that is divine and good in the world."[4]

So you see, according to mystics and others who have given a great deal of time and effort to the study of such things, the child within us is, like God, ageless, timeless and perfect. It is as old and as young as God. It is intimately connected with God. It is a piece of God. It is God.

Overbeliefs

These are profound notions and when we consider them, it is important to be aware that we are dealing with ideas that are called "overbeliefs." Overbeliefs are deeply held opinions or assumptions for which there is no concrete proof. Yet in spite of this, those who hold them are convinced of their credibility and assign them the dominant position in their value systems. These convictions are the essence of faith. "To have faith," wrote the apostle Paul, "is to be sure of things we hope for, to be certain of the things we cannot see."⁵ In addition, these ideas form the foundation of our daily lives. Faith in God is obviously an overbelief, for there is no concrete evidence to convince everyone of his existence.

By the same token, my assumption that I will take my next breath is also an overbelief, for I have absolutely no way of knowing whether I will do so or not. Likewise, my assurance when I go to sleep that I will wake up in the morning is an overbelief. Yet I take such things as breathing and waking up for granted, and if I could not, life would be a nightmare of doubt and uncertainty.

Even though most people tend to think that overbeliefs deal only with relating to higher powers and unseen things, they in fact form the core of every person's existence. Though they cannot be proven, they are held to be true, and they form the very basis of life for those who hold them. Without overbeliefs, life would be impossible, for people would be utterly paralyzed by fear and thus unable to live at all.

It is my contention that the most important assumptions we hold are overbeliefs, for these have the greatest influence on our thinking and behavior. These convictions are not held in the head, but in the heart, and our lives are essentially a demonstration of those things we believe in our hearts, whether we are conscious of them or not. This, I think, is the real meaning of the statement, "For as he thinketh in his heart, so is he."⁶

It has been my observation that as we grow spiritually more is revealed to us, and our convictions change. Ironically, the more we grow, the more we realize that we are returning to the beliefs we held as children.

My own belief system has undergone such a metamorphosis. At my present stage of growth, I believe that all of creation is an expression of the Creator. To me, each tree, flower, sea, mountain, animal and so on is a manifestation of the Source of all being. The same is true of people. All of us are expressions of God. Each of us is the same as, but not identical to, the One who created us.

As one of my own spiritual teachers put it, "I am not saying that I am God, but He is me — and you, and you, and infinitely more."[7]

Meister Eckhart put it more specifically: "God's being is my being . . .. Wherever I am, there is God."[8]

Growing Down

On the matter of spiritual growth, there is uncanny agreement among mystics and children. I will never forget a valuable lesson I learned from my son when he was quite small. Everyone has heard of armchair philosophers. Well, my son, Jason, was a potty-chair philosopher.

By this, I mean that when he sat on his potty someone had to stay with him to keep him company and talk with him.

One night while I was with him, he looked up at me and said quite seriously, "Dad, why don't I be the father and you be the son?"

I was rather taken aback by his statement, so I asked, "Just how do we do that, son?"

Without hesitation, he replied, "It's simple. I'll grow up and be the father. You grow down and be the son."

I was amazed! As incredible as it seemed, I knew that this little boy had just given me the direction that all spiritual growth must take. In spiritual growth, we don't grow up, we grow down to be like little children again — the children of God.

Reflecting on the incident later, I remembered that the carpenter from Nazareth had told his followers that they had to be converted and become as little children if they wanted to enter God's kingdom.[9] It is interesting to note that the Greek word which is translated as "be converted" can also be translated as "to turn around."

Thus, the carpenter was advising his disciples to turn around and grow down. In spiritual growth, we move back toward the reservoir of spiritual wisdom, back in the direction of our innermost selves, back toward the wise child within.

As Eckhart put it, "The soul does not grow by addition, but by subtraction."[10] I have the utmost respect for both mystics and children, and if they say that spiritual growth is a matter of growing down, I cannot disagree.

If we grow down, do we lose something valuable? It would seem so, but happily this is not the case. As a matter of fact, all that we will lose is our arrogance. Growing down reduces the only barrier that blocks us from the loving relationships which will satisfy our thirst for wholeness and that keeps us locked in the dark dungeon of addiction.

That barrier is our human ego. The unrestrained ego is the spoiled brat that lives in all of us, sitting in a high chair, screaming out orders. It is my ego that gets in the car with me, becomes resentful when another car passes me, and insists on taking off faster than the other car at the stoplight.

Some people believe that the ego is bad, but I do not think so. In my opinion, the ego has no comprehension of the concept of selfishness. Thus, it doesn't think of others' needs and desires. It is convinced that what it wants is what everyone wants, that what is best for it is best for all.

The ego is constantly pushing ahead, and it has no thought of ever being stopped. It is frequently dishonest, very adeptly using projection, rationalization and denial. It is insatiable, seeks pleasure constantly, demands complete control over everything and everyone, considers itself to be all-powerful and accepts no limitations. If change is to occur in any person's life, therefore, the ego will have to be deflated.

Deep deflation of the ego has been shown to be a prerequisite to spiritual growth. Twelve-Step groups hold that such deflation occurs when a person "hits bottom" and that until this transpires there is no hope for recovery from addiction. By "hitting bottom" they mean that addicts find themselves in totally untenable situations that they are powerless to change. This, they say, stops the ego and forces it to accept limitations. When the ego is thus reduced, the innermost self is expanded, and as it expands, the innermost self uses common sense and reaches out for a Higher Power. When this happens, recovery begins.

As recovery progresses, there is a continuing decrease in ego and a proportional increase of the innermost self, and on and on. Nothing is added, and nothing is taken away. Yet as time passes, a genuine transformation takes place. Through spiritual growth, people are regenerated by a process that continues to reduce their lower self (ego) while it expands their higher self (the wise child within).

Growing down changes the ratio between the two selves and in so doing transforms the losers of life into winners, making those who were last first. Why do they become first? Because they no longer have the need to be first. In the final analysis, I am persuaded that all spiritual growth is a continuing process of ego deflation, or growth by subtraction, of growing down.

Having thus stated my beliefs, let me turn now and share with you some reflections on the processes involved in the spiritual journey of addiction and recovery.